OFF THE ROAD

AN AMERICAN SKETCHBOOK

Elisha Cooper

VILLARD / NEW YORK

LIBRARY OF CONGRESS CATALOGING-IN-PUBLICATION DATA

Cooper, Elisha.
Off the road: an American sketchbook / Elisha Cooper.—1st ed.
p.   cm.
ISBN 0-679-45586-8
1. Cooper, Elisha—Notebooks, sketchbooks, etc.   2. United States in art.   I. Title.
ND1839.C6684A4   1996
759.13—dc20   96-19381

Random House website address: http://www.randomhouse.com/

Printed in China on acid-free paper

24689753

First Edition

INTERIOR DESIGN BY ROBERT BULL DESIGN

TO MY CAR

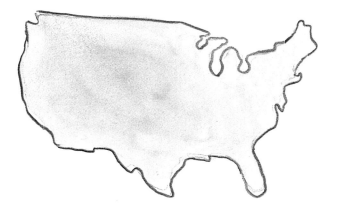

START

I'M GOING TO DRIVE AROUND AMERICA. NEW ENGLAND, THE DEEP SOUTH,
THE PLAINS, ROCKIES, CALIFORNIA COAST, AND BACK.
I'LL GO TO FARMS, FACTORIES, ROADSIDE DINERS, AND BALL GAMES -
JUST PULL OVER WHEN I SEE SOMETHING NEAT. I HAVE A SKETCHBOOK,
MY WATERCOLORS, A SLEEPING BAG, A SET OF ROAD MAPS.
I WANT TO SEE WHAT'S OUT THERE.

DAY 1 - NEW YORK, NEW YORK

PEDESTRIANS SPILL INTO THE STREETS WHILE CABS AND BUSES HONK

AND INCH FORWARD UNTIL THE LIGHT CHANGES GREEN AND THE TRAFFIC FINALLY BREAKS. I'M OFF.

JAZZ PLAYS ON THE RADIO AS THE SKYLINE OF NEW YORK GROWS SMALL.

DAY 1 - SOUTHAMPTON, NEW YORK

I GO HALF THE LENGTH OF LONG ISLAND, HEAD FOR THE BEACH, AND GET

BEHIND THE DUNES, THERE'S A

lots of
white trim

white tely

PUMMELED IN THE SURF.

STEADY PURR OF LAWN MOWERS, HEDGE CLIPPERS, WICKER FIXERS, AND TRASH COLLECTORS.

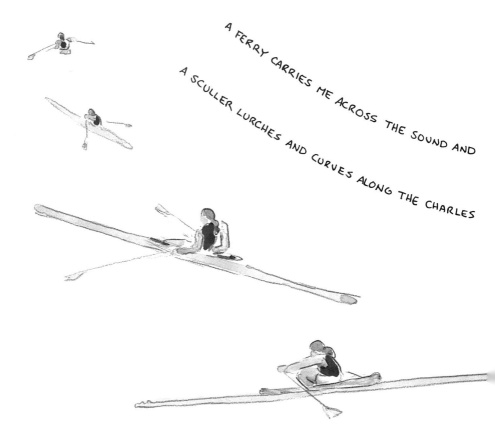

A FERRY CARRIES ME ACROSS THE SOUND AND
A SCULLER LURCHES AND CURVES ALONG THE CHARLES

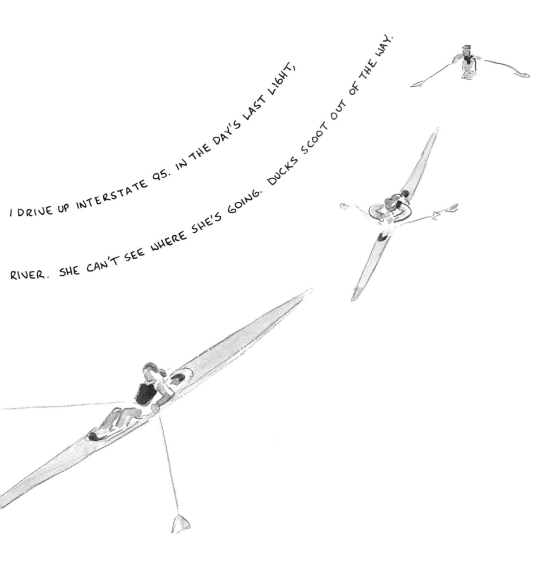

I DRIVE UP INTERSTATE 95. IN THE DAY'S LAST LIGHT,

RIVER. SHE CAN'T SEE WHERE SHE'S GOING. DUCKS SCOOT OUT OF THE WAY.

DAY 2 - FRIENDSHIP, MAINE

BOB O'BRIEN CUTS MY HAIR FOR A CLEAN START TO MY TRIP

JUST TURNED NINETY."

CUSTOMER: "IS THAT RIGHT."

AND TALKS TO THE NEXT MAN IN LINE. O'BRIEN: "I HEAR HIS MOTHER

O'BRIEN: "UH-HUM." CUSTOMER: "IS SHE STILL ALIVE?" O'BRIEN: "YES, SIR."

I BOUNCE AROUND LAKES AND MOUNTAINS TO THE BEN & JERRY'S ICE CREAM FACTORY.
IT'S CHOCK-FULL OF TIE-DYED TOUR GUIDES AND NOTE-TAKING TASTERS
IN FUDGE-STAINED FROCKS – WITH PLYWOOD BLACK-AND-WHITE
COWS ON THE LAWN OUT FRONT.
LATER, I HANG WITH SOME
REAL COWS.

DAY 3— EAST CORINTH, VERMONT

ON ROUTE 113, TWO DRIVERS IN A ROW GIVE ME THE FINGER.
THE THIRD TIME, I REALIZE THE WOMAN IS JUST RAISING HER FINGER.

FOR SALE

DAY 4 - NEW JERSEY TURNPIKE

ROAD CONSTRUCTION 2 LANES

MERGE RIGHT

I DRIVE INTO AMISH COUNTRY. WHILE I'M DRAWING,

A GIRL WHEELS UP BEHIND ME ON A SCOOTER.

HER NAME'S REBECCA AND SHE SAYS MY SKETCH NEEDS WORK.

THEN, WITH A PUSH, SHE'S GONE.

THE GENTLEMAN FROM IOWA IS RANTING: "THE AMERICAN PEOPLE ARE OUTRAGED BY THE DUPLICATIVE

I'M OUTRAGED TOO." PAGES JOKE AND WHISPER. TWO MEMBERS SMOKE CIGARS.

AND UNNECESSARY REPEAL OF THE COMPREHENSIVE PACKAGE PUT FORWARD, AND FRANKLY,

THE ONLY PERSON PAYING ATTENTION IS THE STENOGRAPHER.

DAY 5- WASHINGTON, D.C.

DAY 6 - CHESTERFIELD, VIRGINIA

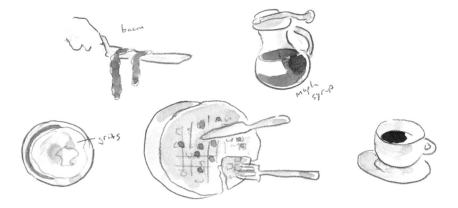

bacon

maple syrup

grits

I LEAVE WASHINGTON AT NIGHT, AND TWO HOURS LATER I'M LOST ON BACK-COUNTY ROADS.
CICADAS LAUGH AT ME. AFTER HITTING THE SAME INTERSECTION THREE TIMES,
I SLEEP IN MY CAR. MORNING COMES, AND A WAFFLE HOUSE SIGN
GUIDES ME BACK TO THE MAIN ROAD
AND BREAKFAST.

toothpick dispenser

dark

tobacco field

yellow

I PULL OVER AT A STEAMY WAREHOUSE SURROUNDED BY PICKUPS.
INSIDE, THERE'S A TOBACCO AUCTION. BUYERS WALK BETWEEN
ROWS OF BURLAP-WRAPPED BAGS – PULLING BACK LEAVES, SMELLING,
TOUCHING – AND HOLD UP THREE OR FOUR FINGERS AS AL GRANGER,
THE AUCTIONEER, CALLS OUT: "TARDY, TARDY, TARDY
. . . FERDY, FERDY, FERDY
. . . FITTY, FITTY, FITTY."

DAY 8- CAPE HATTERAS, NORTH CAROLINA

I LISTEN TO TALK RADIO AS I SPEED ALONG ROUTE 12 IN THE OUTER BANKS

"WHY, SOME PEOPLE JUST DON'T HAVE VALUES, WHAT WE OUGHTA

HE'S INTERRUPTED BY A

ocu toppur

DAY 9 - CHARLESTON, SOUTH CAROLINA

THE MINOR LEAGUE RIVER DOGS ARE PLAYING THE ALABAMA POLE CATS.
FOUL BALLS JUMP OUT OF THE STADIUM, DIP INTO THE PARKING LOT,
PLONK OFF THE ROOFS OF CARS, AND ROLL UNDERNEATH THE WHEELS,
WHERE TWO BAGGY-SHORTED KIDS CHASE AFTER THEM.
AFTER FIVE INNINGS THEY HAVE TWELVE BALLS.

IT'S EIGHT IN THE MORNING WHEN I PULL INTO "THE BEST MILITARY INSTALLATION

IN THE WORLD." THEY'VE GOT A GOLF COURSE, A SHOOTING RANGE, AN EXPLOSIVE-

CARGO AREA, A PERFORMANCE ART CENTER, A THRIFT SHOP, A FLORIST, AND THE LONE

DENTAL CLINIC. A GROUP OF SOLDIERS CLIPS THE LAWNS, KEEPING EVERYTHING PRETTY.

DAY 11 - MIAMI BEACH, FLORIDA

AN ALL-DAY DRIVE THROUGH ORANGE GROVES AND WAL-MARTS

BATHERS LATHER THEMSELVES WITH BODY OIL AND SUNTAN LOTION,

LEADS ME TO SOUTH FLORIDA AND ITS BEACHES.

TRYING HARD NOT TO GET CAUGHT CHECKING OUT OTHER PEOPLE'S BODIES.

IT'S WAY PAST TIME TO CLEAN MY CLOTHES. I GO TO A LAUNDROMAT ON GEN. MAXIMILIO SOMEZ AVENUE WHERE MERENGUE'S PLAYING. MEN AND WOMEN MOVE THEIR BODIES AND THEIR LAUNDRY TO THE BEAT, BOBBING HEADS WHILE FOLDING SHEETS, SWINGING BUTTS WHILE SHIFTING CLOTHES TO THE DRYER, HIP-SWISHING DOWN THE AISLES.

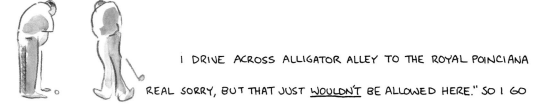

I DRIVE ACROSS ALLIGATOR ALLEY TO THE ROYAL POINCIANA

REAL SORRY, BUT THAT JUST <u>WOULDN'T</u> BE ALLOWED HERE." SO I GO

GOLF COURSE. WHEN I START SKETCHING, THE PRESSED-KHAKI GUARD SAYS, "I'M

TO THE PUBLIC COURSE AND DRAW PUTTERS FROM BEHIND A PINK STUCCO FENCE.

DAY 13 - SHORTER, ALABAMA

NEXT TO THE SWEET CANAAN MISSIONARY BAPTIST CHURCH, A. L. JENKINS SITS ROCKING ON HIS PORCH. EVERY FIVE MINUTES, HIS GRANDDAUGHTER SLAMS THROUGH THE SCREEN DOOR, GRABS HIS LEG, AND LOOKS OUT AT ME

WHEN SHE GOES BACK, I HEAR HER VOICE RATTLING INSIDE THE HOUSE.

DAY 14 - PHILADELPHIA, TENNESSEE

A HAWK BALANCES ON A BARBED WIRE FENCE BY THE SIDE OF THE ROAD,

STARES BEHIND HER, THEN FLAPS DOWN TO GRAB DINNER.

DAY 15 - MOSS POINT, MISSISSIPPI

I STOP AT AMERICAN LEGION HALL NO. 243 ON A POORLY LIT ROAD. A MINUTE LATER,

NUMBERS, WE STAMP GAME CARDS WITH RED MARKERS, GROAN WHEN SOMEONE

I'M PLAYING BINGO WITH FRANK THE CALLER AND THREE HUNDRED WOMEN. HE SHOUTS

YELLS "BINGO!" THEN FLIP SHEETS WITH AN "OH WELL" RUSTLE TO THE NEXT ROUND.

IN FRONT OF THE OLD JAZZ HALL, THE CAJUNDALE STRIP SHOW, THE BURLESQUE DANCE CLUB, AND THE NOVELTY CONDOM SHOP, A WORKER SPRAYS THE STREETS. BUT SHE CAN'T WASH AWAY THE SWEET SMELL OF THROW-UP FROM THE NIGHT BEFORE.

A BUG FLIES AROUND INSIDE MY CAR. I TRY TO THWACK IT WITH A MAP. BEFORE LONG THERE'S ANOTHER, THEN ANOTHER. FEELING OUTNUMBERED,

light

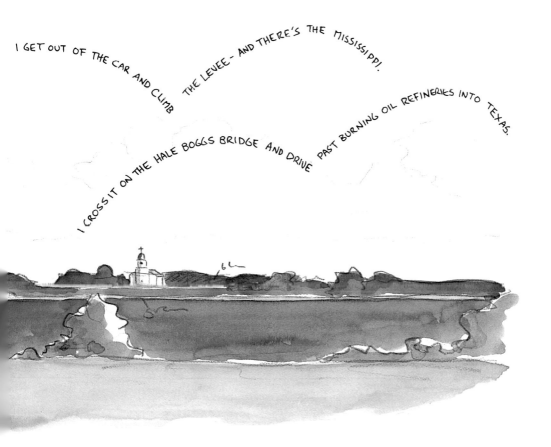

I GET OUT OF THE CAR AND CLIMB THE LEVEE – AND THERE'S THE MISSISSIPPI.

I CROSS IT ON THE HALE BOGGS BRIDGE AND DRIVE PAST BURNING OIL REFINERIES INTO TEXAS.

AT THE CLAYTON HOMES HOUSING PROJECT I HEAR A FAMILIAR
BELL. KIDS, GRIPPING COINS AND CRUMPLED BILLS, SPRINT OUT
ALLEYWAYS, RUSH OUT DOORS, AND CONVERGE ON THE UDDER
GOODNESS ICE CREAM TRUCK. JOSEPH DIXON, NINE AND GANGLY,
PEERS OVER MY SHOULDER AS I SKETCH — "WHAT YOU DOIN'
<u>NOW</u>?" — DRIPPING LEMON FROM HIS SNOW CONE.

DAY 18- FORT WORTH, TEXAS

FRIDAY NIGHT AT BILLY BOB'S, THE HUGEST HONKY-TONK THERE IS. MUSIC PUMPS

ON A DANCE FLOOR SURROUNDED BY A WOODEN CORRAL, TWO-STEPPERS CIRCLE BENEATH

PAST THREE NEON-COVERED BARS AND ONE MECHANICAL BULL THAT DOESN'T WORK.

A DISCO "BALL" THAT'S SHAPED LIKE A SADDLE. I FEEL NAKED WITHOUT A COWBOY HAT.

DAY 19 - ELECTRA, TEXAS

DRIVING THROUGH DESERTED OIL FIELDS, LISTENING TO COUNTRY, WRITING

"THAT AIN'T MY TRUCK IN HER DRIVEWAY,"

I SEE A SIGN BY THE SIDE OF THE ROAD:

DOWN MY FAVORITES: "YOU SAY IT BEST WHEN YOU SAY NOTHING AT ALL,"

AND "OUT OF GAS, JUST MY LUCK."

"VASECTOMY REVERSAL - EXIT 173C"

I STOP FOR A BURGER AT RED'S DRIVE-IN.
FIVE MEN SIT AT FIVE DIFFERENT BOOTHS
AND TALK IN THE SAME CONVERSATION. THEY YAK ABOUT FRIDAY'S GAME,
THE UPCOMING CHURCH PICNIC, THE DOWNFALL OF SOCIAL SECURITY.
I JOIN IN, AND WE DISCUSS TORNADOES.

DAY 20- ENID, OKLAHOMA

I'M MOTORING ALONG A STRAIGHT GRAVEL ROAD WHEN I HEAR SHOOTING. I PULL OVER QUICK, BUT IT'S JUST THE ENID ELKS GUN CLUB

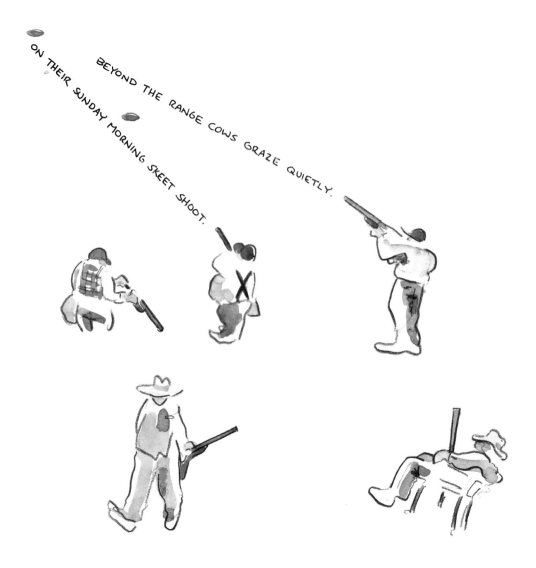

BEYOND THE RANGE COWS GRAZE QUIETLY.

ON THEIR SUNDAY MORNING SKEET SHOOT.

DAY 21 - CULLISON, KANSAS

orange

gold

I
STOP
NEAR A
"JESUS IS LORD"
SIGN, HOP THE FENCE,
AND WALK INTO WHEAT FIELDS
THAT SWIRL AROUND ME AND REACH TO THE HORIZON.

DAY 21 - DODGE CITY, KANSAS

AT NIGHT, THEY ARE SLEEPING GIANTS. THEY MAKE

THEIR YELLOW EYES BLINK, THEIR STOMACHS RUMBLE.

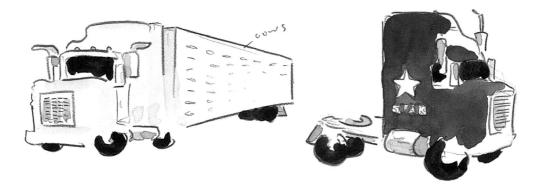

THEIR BEDS AT THE REST STOP, WHERE THEY LIE IN ROWS.

IN THE MORNING, THEY GROWL AWAKE AND ROLL AWAY.

YELLOW BUTTERFLIES FLIT ACROSS THE ROAD AND SMACK AGAINST MY WINDSHIELD. THROUGH THE

GOOP ON THE GLASS I SEE A MAN IN THE BREAKDOWN LANE TRYING TO HITCHHIKE BACK TO KANSAS.

DAY 23-CANYONLANDS NATIONAL PARK, UTAH

I CURL UP IN MY SLEEPING BAG BY THE SIDE OF THE ROAD. IT'S

TWENTY MINUTES. I SEE NOTHING BUT HAZY CONSTELLATIONS AND THE OCCASIONAL

DARK AND SILENT AND COLD. A SEMI SWOOSHES BY EVERY
SHOOTING STAR SLITTING THE SKY. I WAKE UP AMONG CANYONS.

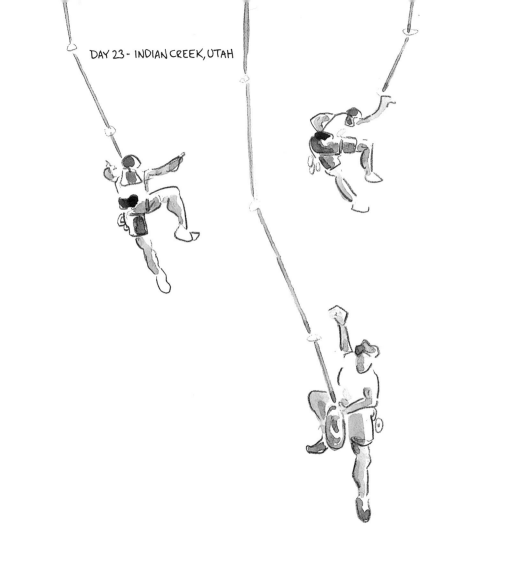

DAY 23 - INDIAN CREEK, UTAH

HEADING SOUTH THROUGH GLOWING MESAS, I PULL OVER AT A DIRT LOT NEXT TO AN OLD SPANISH CHURCH WHERE THREE KIDS PLAY SOCCER. DUSK SETS IN, BUT THE BALL KEEPS MOVING BACK AND FORTH, OCCASIONALLY THOMPING INTO THE SIDE OF THE CHURCH.

DAY 25 – SECOND MESA, ARIZONA

yellow mtns.

WHEN I STOP AT A GAS STATION ON THE HOPI INDIAN RESERVATION, FIVE DOGS SWAGGER OVER TO

GREET ME, CHECK ME OUT, LICK MY FACE, LIE IN THE SHADE UNDER THE CAR, AND PEE ON THE WHEELS.

AFTER WATCHING BLACKJACK AT CAESARS PALACE, I GO TO A 24-HOUR DRIVE-THROUGH CHAPEL

THE GROOM WEARS NIKES.

HIS BRIDE CHEWS GUM AND BLOWS BUBBLES.

DAY 27- ENCINITAS, CALIFORNIA

IT'S 118 DEGREES AT NIGHT. I POUR WATER OVER MY HEAD AS I DRIVE THROUGH

OF THE PACIFIC. I SPEED UP, PARK, SPRINT ACROSS THE SAND

oil well

THE DESERT. THE SUN RISES BEHIND ME AND I SEE THE BLUE BAND
- TEARING OFF MY CLOTHES AS I RUN — AND SPLASH OUT INTO THE WATER.

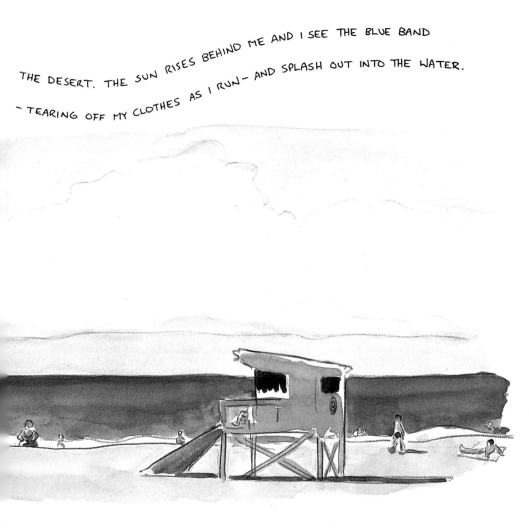

I'M AT THE DOWNTOWN GREYHOUND BUS TERMINAL. MIGUEL LOREN SNORES, THEN WAKES AND GRIPES

ABOUT THE DELAYS: "MAN, THESE BUSES IS SLOWER THAN MY AUNT IN YUMA. AND SHE'S SLOW."

ANOTHER MAN SMOKES, RESTS ON HIS CRUTCHES, AND STARES AT HIS FEET.

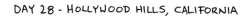

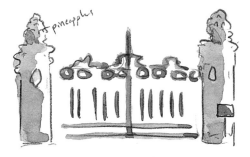

pineapples

lions

dog

ROLLERBLADERS GROOVE TO DISCO.

I DRINK TWO ICED TEAS, BUY GAS, DRIVE NORTH.

ROWS OF ARTICHOKES. ROWS OF WORKERS. POP MUSIC FLOATS ACROSS THE FIELD

MI CHICA, NO ME QUIERE, MI CHICA, TE QUIERO . . ."

FROM A TRANSPORTATION BUS AND ITS WHEELED PORTA POTTY: "MI CHICA, TE QUIERO,

THE "TCK, TCK, TCK" OF A SPURTING WATER SPRINKLER PROVIDES THE BASS.

DAY 30 - BIG SUR, CALIFORNIA

LEAVING ROUTE 1 TO WHIZZING CYCLISTS AND PUTT-PUTTING VWs,

I GLIDE THROUGH SHADOWS CAST BY CYPRESS TREES DOWN TO PFEIFFER BEACH.

A PAIR OF OTTERS RIDE THE CREST OF THE WAVES, CRACKING MUSSELS OFF THEIR BELLIES.

AT THE SUSHI BAR I WATCH MICHAEL NIMURA'S HANDS SNATCH A SHEET OF SEAWEED, COAT IT WITH

WASABI, SPREAD IT WITH RICE, SLAP IT WITH TUNA, ROLL IT, BEND IT, CUT IT QUICK WITH A KNIFE. DONE. ON TO THE NEXT.

DAY 31 – SAN FRANCISCO, CALIFORNIA

I SKETCH THE BAY FROM THE TOP OF NOB HILL. TO THE NORTH I SEE A WET BANK

OF FOG SLUMPING TOWARD ME.   TEN MINUTES LATER I'VE LOST   MY VIEW.

NO PLACE TO HIDE MY SKETCHBOOK AT THE NUDIST HARBIN HOT SPRINGS.

cards

yoga

touching

hiking

SELF, INNER PEACE" WORKSHOP. ALL'S PAYABLE BY CREDIT CARD.

SO I HANG IN THE MINERAL WATER POOL, WATCH COUPLES DO WATSU

(WATER YOGA), CHILL AT THE JUICE BAR, AND READ NOTICES FOR THE "INNER

INTERSTATE 5'S DUSTY VALLEYS GIVE WAY TO THE FIR-ROUNDED HILLS OF THE CASCADES AND SMALL-TOWN PAPER MILLS.

THE SMELL OF CUT WOOD DRIFTS ACROSS THE ROAD
AS I SKETCH WORKERS HAMMERING ON A ROOF.

DAY 34- SEATTLE, WASHINGTON

I SHOW UP FOR A PIONEER SQUARE POETRY SLAM, BUT NOTHING'S HAPPENING. IS IT CANCELED? NO ONE KNOWS WHAT'S UP. WOULD-BE POETS HUNKER OUTSIDE ON THE SIDEWALK, MEMORIZING, SWEARING.

DAY 34 – BALLARD, WASHINGTON

SALMON FLAPPING THROUGH THE AIR. SOMETIMES HEADLESS.

FLYING FISH. FOURTEEN-POUND

EVERY FIFTH FISH OR SO IS JUGGLED.

MOVING FROM BEDS OF ICE TO WAXED PAPER TO SCALES TO PACKAGES.

I LEAVE THE MARKET AND DRIVE TO THE DOCKS IN THE RAIN.

DAY 35 - COEUR D'ALENE, IDAHO

I WIND ALONG RIVERS AND CURVE THROUGH MOUNTAINS ON INTERSTATE 90. A FLOCK OF

BIKERS IN BLACK JACKETS ROARS BY MY CAR. I'M A GOOSE SURROUNDED BY COOL CROWS.

DAY 36 – LEADORE, IDAHO

FIREFIGHTER RAYMOND SNEAD LOUNGES OUTSIDE
THE U.S. FOREST SERVICE STATION, SMOKING.
I ASK IF THERE ARE ANY FIRES TODAY AND HE SAYS, "YUP."

I ASK IF HE KNOWS WHERE AND HE SAYS, "NOPE." I STOP
AT THE ONE STORE IN TOWN, SEND A POSTCARD,
LOOK AT THE TAXIDERMY, DRINK A BEER.

DAY 37 - YELLOWSTONE NATIONAL PARK, WYOMING

chairs

YELLOW

POWERRIVER

yellow

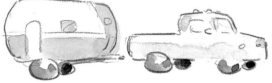

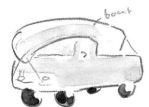

boat

blue

blue,
lin.

DAY 37 - MOOSE JUNCTION, WYOMING

RUBBER
RAFTS
LOOK
LIKE
HUGE
FLOATING
PANCAKES
COVERED WITH
RED LIFE-JACKETED BERRIES
AS THEY FLOP DOWN THE RAPIDS
OF THE SNAKE RIVER. ONE OF THE BERRIES
FALLS OFF AND BOBS TO THE BANK.

DAY 38 - LIVINGSTON, MONTANA

I DESCEND THROUGH MOUNTAINS ON A SUNDAY MORNING AND

THAT I, TOO, AM A SPECIAL EMBODIMENT OF CHRIST JESUS AND THAT I MUST CLEANSE

LISTEN TO A CHURCH SERVICE ON THE RADIO. THE MINISTER SAYS MYSELF OF THE IMPURITIES OF THE SOUL. I PULL INTO TOWN AND GET A LUBE JOB.

DAY 39 - MISSOULA, MONTANA

DRIVING NORTH ALONG THE BITTERROOT RIVER, I STOP

AT A RODEO AND WATCH THE "MUTTON BUSTIN'." TODDLERS TAKE THEIR CHANCES

WITH SOME OF THE BADDEST SHEEP IN THE COUNTY. WHEN DUMPED IN THE DUST SOME OF THESE COWPOKES CRY.

BUT AFTER A HUG FROM MOM THEY'RE READY TO RIDE AGAIN.

DAY 40 - ALICE, NORTH DAKOTA

COWS
DOT THE
FIELDS ON BOTH
SIDES OF THE ROAD.
I SLOW DOWN, STICK MY HEAD
OUT THE WINDOW, AND MOO. A
FEW OF THE MORE CURIOUS CALVES

MOO BACK AND TROT AFTER ME.
        MOST JUST TILT THEIR HEADS AND STARE.

DAY 41 - MISSION, SOUTH DAKOTA

NORMAN TOKALA AND HIS TRACTOR GRUMBLE UP AND DOWN IN ROWS, GIVING BIRTH

BALES OF HAY. ON THE HORIZON

FROM ROLLING GRAY CLOUDS TO THE FIELDS BELOW.

PERIODICALLY TO ROUND, BOUND

ABOVE THE ROSEBUD INDIAN RESERVATION, LIGHTNING DANCES

THE TRACTOR SPEEDS UP.

DAY 42 - GOOD THUNDER, MINNESOTA

I SKETCH A FARM ON COUNTY ROAD 13. AROUND THE BEND I SEE A FERRIS WHEEL, SO I GO AND CHECK OUT THE COUNTY FAIR. THERE'S A TUPPERWARE BOOTH, A CHEESE CURD BOOTH, A BOOTH FOR THE REPUBLICAN PARTY, A BOOTH FOR GIANT VEGETABLES, AND ONE FOR A SNAPPY NEW MACHINE THAT MONITORS HOG-FEED CONSUMPTION.

JORDAN HENRY TAKES THE PABST BLUE
RIBBON FACTORY TOUR TO FINISH IT.
HE PATIENTLY LISTENS TO AN HOUR OF FACTS ABOUT THE
BOILING POINT OF HOPS BEFORE GETTING HIS TWO FREE
DRAFTS. BURPING AT HIS TABLE, HE SMILES: "WOW, CAN'T
<u>WAIT</u> TO COME BACK TOMORROW."

DAY 45 - CHICAGO BOARD OF TRADE, ILLINOIS

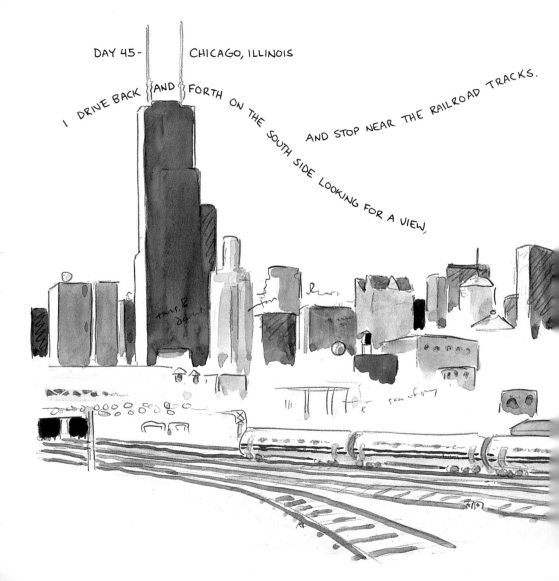

DAY 45 —   CHICAGO, ILLINOIS

I DRIVE BACK AND FORTH ON THE SOUTH SIDE LOOKING FOR A VIEW, AND STOP NEAR THE RAILROAD TRACKS.

TWO MEN COME OUT OF THE DINER ON THE CORNER TO ASK IF I'M LOST.

AT THE BOTTOM OF TRAIN CARS THERE'S GRAFFITI: "OFF TO CALI," "YO JANE," "SHAZZAM!"

RAP BOOMS ACROSS THE ROAD FROM THE USED-CAR LOT
AND RATTLES MY WINDOWS. A SALESWOMAN FLIPS A PAIR
OF KEYS IN HER HAND, THEN ADDS A TENNIS BALL
AND STARTS JUGGLING.

DAY 47 - MUSKEGON, MICHIGAN

white
light to

I HOLD MY SKETCHBOOK OVER MY HEAD AND SWIM OUT TO A SANDBAR.   TO DRAW

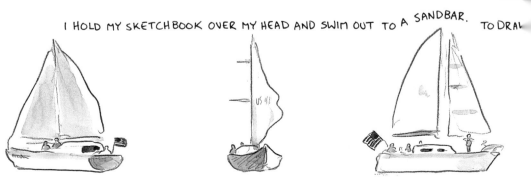

THE SHORE I STAND ON THE TIPS OF MY TOES IN THE WAVES. BEHIND ME I HEAR THE FAINT CALLS OF WEEKENDING SAILBOATERS.

DAY 48 - DETROIT, MICHIGAN

I'M TOLD I HAVE TO GET PERMISSION FROM THE LABOR
RELATIONS BOARD TO GO ON A TOUR OF THE AUTO PLANT.
"AND THAT WILL TAKE A COUPLE OF WEEKS OR MORE," SAYS TASHA
HIGGS FROM HER PLASTIC BOOTH. SO I SIT ON A CURB INSTEAD
AND SKETCH WORKERS ON THEIR COFFEE BREAK.

DRIVING ALONG CUYAHOGA FALLS AVENUE I HEAR WHISTLES

CHEEKS TO SPIT AT EACH OTHER.

AND DRINK GALLONS, SAVING JUST ENOUGH IN THEIR

AND GRUNTS BEFORE I ACTUALLY SEE   THE EARLY MORNING HIGH SCHOOL FOOTBALL PRACTICE. DURING BREAKS, PLAYERS GATHER AT THE WATER FOUNTAIN

IT'S CLOSING TIME. JENNY LING MOPS THE FLOOR, CREATING TIDAL WAVES AS SHE PUSHES WATER TO THE FAR CORNERS OF THE RESTAURANT. I PUSH EAST ON INTERSTATE 76, AND THE MOON FOLLOWS OVER MY SHOULDER.

DAY 50- NEW YORK, NEW YORK

THE NEW YORK SKYLINE REAPPEARS. I CROSS THE HUDSON AND GO TO CENTRAL PARK WHERE I FIND ROLLERBLADERS

SWERVING AROUND A YOUNG TROMBONIST OOMPA-OOMPAING ON A PATH. HIS BLOWING JOINS HORNS,

SHOUTS, RUMBLING PLANES, AND BECOMES ONE VOICE IN A CHORUS.

FINISH

MY TRIP IS OVER. I SIT IN THE PARK AS THE SUN GOES DOWN AND THINK OF WHAT IT MUST LOOK LIKE ON BATHERS IN FLORIDA, TWO-STEPPERS DANCING IN TEXAS, KIDS RIDING SHEEP IN MONTANA, OR WORKERS SWEATING IN OREGON. THIS COUNTRY IS HUGE - WIDE VIEWS, PACKED CITIES - BUT SOMETIMES IT'S INCREDIBLY SMALL: ALIVE, COLORFUL, PERSONAL.

AMERICA IS WHERE YOU ARE.

ABOUT THE AUTHOR

ELISHA COOPER PLAYED FOOTBALL AT YALE, THEN WORKED
AS A MESSENGER AT *THE NEW YORKER* MAGAZINE. HE IS
THE AUTHOR OF *A YEAR IN NEW YORK* AND IS TWENTY-FIVE
YEARS OLD. THIS IS HIS SECOND BOOK.